ULTIMATE
NASCAR
Road Trip

By Heather Rule

**ULTIMATE SPORTS
ROAD TRIPS**

SportsZone

An Imprint of Abdo Publishing
abdobooks.com

ABDOBOOKS.COM

Published by Abdo Publishing, a division of ABDO, PO Box 398166, Minneapolis, Minnesota 55439.
Copyright © 2019 by Abdo Consulting Group, Inc. International copyrights reserved in all countries.
No part of this book may be reproduced in any form without written permission from the publisher.
SportsZone™ is a trademark and logo of Abdo Publishing.

Printed in the United States of America, North Mankato, Minnesota
092018
012019

Cover Photo: Logan Whitton/NKP/AP Images
Interior Photos: Logan Whitton/NKP/AP Images, 1, 27, 43; John Raoux/AP Images, 4–5; Tony Gutierrez/
AP Images, 7, 8; Action Sports Photography/Shutterstock Images, 11, 18–19, 28, 35, 44, 45; Bill Elliott/AP
Images, 12–13; Todd Warshaw/AP Images, 15; Phelan M. Ebenhack/AP Images, 17; Jerry Markland/Getty
Images for NASCAR/Getty Images Sport/Getty Images, 21; Drew Hallowell/Getty Images Sport/Getty
Images, 23; Jerry Markland/Getty Images Sport/Getty Images, 24; Jared C. Tilton/Getty Images Sport/
Getty Images, 31; RacingOne/ISC Archives/Getty Images, 32; Rusty Jarrett/Getty Images for NASCAR/
Getty Images Sport/Getty Images, 37; Todd Warshaw/Getty Images Sport/Getty Images, 39; Rich Barnes/
Cal Sport Media/Newscom, 40–41

Editor: Bradley Cole
Series Designer: Melissa Martin

Library of Congress Control Number: 2018949186

Publisher's Cataloging-in-Publication Data

Names: Rule, Heather, author.
Title: Ultimate NASCAR road trip / by Heather Rule.
Description: Minneapolis, Minnesota : Abdo Publishing, 2019 | Series: Ultimate sports road trips |
    Includes online resources and index.
Identifiers: ISBN 9781532117534 (lib. bdg.) | ISBN 9781532170393 (ebook)
Subjects: LCSH: Sports arenas--Juvenile literature. | Sports spectators--Juvenile literature. | NASCAR
    racing--Juvenile literature. | National Association for Stock Car Auto Racing (U.S.)--Juvenile
    literature.
Classification: DDC 796.720973--dc23

TABLE OF CONTENTS

INTRODUCTION
START YOUR ENGINES! 4

CHAPTER 1
TEXAS MOTOR SPEEDWAY 6

CHAPTER 2
TALLADEGA SUPERSPEEDWAY 10

CHAPTER 3
DAYTONA
INTERNATIONAL SPEEDWAY 16

CHAPTER 4
CHARLOTTE MOTOR SPEEDWAY 22

CHAPTER 5
BRISTOL MOTOR SPEEDWAY 26

CHAPTER 6
MARTINSVILLE SPEEDWAY 30

CHAPTER 7
RICHMOND
INTERNATIONAL RACEWAY 34

CHAPTER 8
WATKINS GLEN INTERNATIONAL 38

MAP 44   ONLINE RESOURCES. . . 47

GLOSSARY. 46   INDEX 48

MORE INFORMATION. . . 47   ABOUT THE AUTHOR . . 48

Start Your ENGINES!

Through the years, many sporting events have been widely televised so fans can watch their favorite sport at home. But sometimes there's just no comparison to actually being there in person. That's especially true for auto racing. The sights and sounds of National Association for Stock Car Auto Racing (NASCAR) are hard to beat. The series schedule includes a variety of tracks each season that fans can experience with thousands of other racing enthusiasts.

NASCAR was officially started back in 1948 by Bill France Sr. The Daytona 500 is its most prestigious race. Most of the tracks in NASCAR are some kind of oval. The largest ovals are found in tracks called superspeedways. Some tracks have long straightaways heading into corners, whereas others invite tight racing with high-banked turns.

Whether a fan is enjoying the history and excitement of a place such as Daytona, waiting for "the big one" at Talladega, or taking in the twists and turns of a sprawling road course such as Watkins Glen, the tracks on the NASCAR circuit have a lot to offer. Now strap in for the ultimate NASCAR road trip.

The fun of pre-race tailgating parties continues into the actual events, filling NASCAR raceways with excitement and energy.

TEXAS
MOTOR
SPEEDWAY

Texas Motor Speedway is a relatively new track, but it isn't lacking spirit. Fans fill the infield with RVs and cars to camp and tailgate before the race. Grills and smokers line the infield and several designated camping areas outside the track. In total there are more than 8,500 camping spots across the 1,500 acres (6 sq km) of Texas Motor Speedway. Good food and great races are always easy to find here. The 1.5-mile (2.4-km) oval speedway hosts two NASCAR races every year.

In 1997 Jeff Burton won the first 500-mile (805-km) NASCAR race at the speedway in front of more than 200,000 fans. The track has tall grandstands along the main straightaway to house the

FUN FACT

Texas Motor Speedway opened in 1997, and that year the facility hosted concerts including RockFest and CountryFest.

TEXAS MOTOR SPEEDWAY

Fort Worth, Texas

Date Opened: 1997
Capacity: 181,655 total estimated capacity
(128,655 permanent seating)

second-most fans of any track in America. The speedway installed
several upgrades through the years, making the track safer for
drivers and more fun for fans but decreasing the capacity. New
barriers called SAFER (steel and foam energy reduction) were
installed around the track walls. They help lessen the impact
for drivers in crashes. The speedway also added Pit Stop Park in

Elliott Sadler just barely stole the win from Kasey Kahne in the closest victory at Texas Motor Speedway.

2011 to give fans more room to tailgate. New restaurants and areas for eating in the infield have also been added. And if fans want a photo-op, there is even a larger-than-life bobblehead doll. With improved cell-phone reception, fans can also post their pictures to social media. Wi-Fi is also available for fans both on the track and in the parking lot.

The closest margin of victory at the speedway during a NASCAR race came in April 2004. Rookie driver Kasey Kahne in his No. 9 car charged through the field of cars in a few laps to take the lead for 148 laps. But it was Elliott Sadler who had the luck that day in his M&M's-sponsored car. He took over the lead after a caution period of pit stops for other drivers, including Kahne. Sadler and Kahne were wheel to wheel after the fourth turn on the final lap. Sadler crossed the line first by just 0.028 seconds.

2 TALLADEGA
SUPERSPEEDWAY

NASCAR is often known for its big wrecks. Many of these crashes happen at Talladega Superspeedway in Alabama. The 2.66-mile (4.28-km) oval is known as "the world's fastest racetrack." When it opened in 1969, drivers worried their tires wouldn't be able to handle the fast speeds, which can top 200 miles per hour (322 km/h).

Talladega is a sister track to Daytona International Speedway, meaning Talladega is similar but a little bigger. The tri-oval has 33 degrees of steep banking in the turns, helping cars keep their speeds up. Talladega gets so fast that NASCAR makes teams install restrictor plates on their cars to limit their speed. In 2004 Rusty Wallace finished a pre-race lap averaging 216 miles per hour (348 km/h). Wallace hit

FUN FACT

Buddy Baker was the first driver to push a stock car to more than 200 miles per hour (321.9 km/h) when he took a lap at Talladega at 200.447 miles per hour (322.588 km/h) in a winged Dodge Daytona car on March 24, 1970.

TALLADEGA SUPERSPEEDWAY

Talladega, Alabama

Date Opened: 1969
Capacity: 78,000

 The fastest laps and largest wrecks happen at Talladega Superspeedway.

a top speed of 228 miles per hour (367 km/h) on the lap. Even with restrictor plates, the drivers find ways to hit the fastest speeds in all of NASCAR at Talladega. With so many cars on the track at high speeds, drivers race side by side just inches apart. Drivers will often "bump draft," nudging the car ahead of them for a little push. It speeds up the front car and drags along the car behind it as well.

One of the biggest crashes in the track's history came on lap 133 in the 2005 edition of a race called the Aaron's 499. Drivers had been cautioned against bump drafting before the race. Jimmie Johnson drifted upward on the track. Dale Earnhardt Jr. bumped Mike Wallace from behind, and Wallace hit the wall then lost control. Wallace and Johnson then collided. The crash created a chain reaction, causing a 25-car pileup, the second-biggest wreck in NASCAR history. Luckily, no one was seriously injured. It took 43 minutes to clean up the track and repair the barriers. The largest wreck in NASCAR history, a 27-car pileup, also happened at Talladega just two years earlier.

Then there's the Talladega Curse. Some people think the racetrack is haunted. In 1973 Bobby Isaac pulled his car off the track, saying he heard a ghostly voice threatening him and telling him to get out of his car. Driver Larry Smith was killed in a crash during that race. Isaac didn't race again that season.

FUN FACT

Bill Elliott set a record that's been untouched for years. He drove his Ford 212.809 miles per hour (342.483 km/h) on a pole lap at Talladega on April 30, 1987. It's the fastest pole lap in NASCAR history.

Jimmie Johnson earned one of his many wins by the slightest margin of victory in NASCAR history in the 2011 Aaron's 499. Johnson got a late push from his teammate, Dale Earnhardt Jr. The bump put Johnson across the finish line first, just 0.002 seconds ahead of Clint Bowyer. It matched the closest finish since NASCAR started using electronic timing in 1993.

At its largest, Talladega Superspeedway could pack 175,000 screaming race fans in the stands. That made it the largest track

Jimmie Johnson (48) made NASCAR history when Dale Earnhardt Jr. (88) bumped him across the finish line just before Clint Bowyer (33).

in NASCAR. After renovations it now seats 97,000 fewer fans. But that doesn't mean Talladega is any less grand. A parade called "Big One on the Blvd" takes place on the track the day before the Talladega 250 and General Tire 200.

3 DAYTONA INTERNATIONAL SPEEDWAY

S tock cars used to race partially on the sandy shores of Daytona Beach, Florida, on a 3.2-mile (5.15-km) road and beach course starting in 1936. But when NASCAR founder Bill France Sr. saw the growth in the area after World War II (1939–1945), he decided to build a speedway.

FUN FACT

Janet Guthrie became the first woman to race in the Daytona 500 in 1977. She was the highest-placing rookie, finishing in twelfth place.

Daytona International Speedway in Daytona Beach is home to NASCAR's most prestigious race. The Daytona 500, also known as NASCAR's Super Bowl and the "Great American Race," takes place each February. NASCAR also runs a 400-mile (644-km) race at Daytona each year around the Fourth of July weekend.

DAYTONA INTERNATIONAL SPEEDWAY

Daytona Beach, Florida

Date Opened: 1959
Capacity: 101,000

 Some of the best races in NASCAR history have happened at the three-lane-wide Daytona track.

Daytona's high-banked oval allows for faster speeds and a better view for fans. In the middle of the infield is Lake Lloyd, a long, rectangular strip of water that was created during construction when workers had to dig up tons of soil to make the track banking.

Besides the track itself, the food also makes Daytona special. Fans can chow down on prime rib sandwiches, fusion tacos, pizza, and even pitas. And many fans show up early to camp out in the famous 180-acre (73-ha) infield. Camping lakeside at Lake Lloyd is

just one of the great amenities fans can experience before seeing a race on the famous three-wide track.

The speedway opened on February 20, 1959, for the qualifying for the inaugural Daytona 500. Lee Petty was racing a brand-new 1959 Oldsmobile. He battled on the track with Johnny Beauchamp in his 1959 Thunderbird. They dueled and exchanged the lead over the final 30 laps. Each driver thought he had won the race as they crossed the line side by side. Beauchamp was declared the unofficial winner. But three days later, after looking at photo and video evidence of the close finish, NASCAR named Petty the rightful winner.

One of the most notable moments at Daytona is also one of the most tragic. Legendary driver Dale Earnhardt Sr. tried 19 times to win the 500 before finally doing it in 1998. But three years later in 2001, Earnhardt hit the wall head-on and was also hit by another car on the final turn of the race. He died from his injuries. After Earnhardt's death, NASCAR implemented rule changes designed to increase drivers' safety. Each driver was required to use more safety equipment, such as a HANS (head and neck support) device that attaches to the driver's helmet.

It may have taken Earnhardt 19 years to reach victory lane at the Daytona 500, but his son didn't face such a dry spell. Dale Earnhardt Jr. started from the second row in the 2004 Daytona 500 and passed Tony Stewart with just 19 laps left. Junior took the lead and held off Stewart to win his first Daytona 500.

FUN FACT

Daytona is also home to North America's most prestigious sports car race, the Rolex 24 Hours at Daytona. It's a 24-hour marathon race with no breaks. Drivers on each team take turns driving the same car. Legendary drivers have been running there since the event started in 1962.

Daytona features some of the best views and experiences in all of NASCAR with wild racing, Lake Lloyd in the infield, and plenty of camping.

The speedway has been renovated multiple times, including in 1998 when lighting was installed. The Daytona Rising project, a three-year, $400-million project to improve the fan experience, started in 2013. Highlights include redesigned fan entrances, more comfortable spectator seating, and more access to concessions and restrooms. With the importance of its races, the wide track that allows cars to race three wide, and the camping and food, there is no other racetrack like Daytona International Speedway.

4 CHARLOTTE
MOTOR
SPEEDWAY

Charlotte Motor Speedway prides itself on being known as "The Greatest Place to See the Race." The 1.5-mile (2.4-km) superspeedway has placed the fan experience at the top of the list. Track owners have made improvements to give fans a better and more enjoyable time at the race. The Fan Zone features interactive games, tents for fans to buy gear, and much more. The Play Zone includes a bounce house, a petting zoo, and face painting for kids.

Charlotte was designed and opened by O. Bruton Smith, a car dealer and short track promoter, and racer Curtis Turner. The duo

FUN FACT

The movies *Days of Thunder, Speedway*, and *Talladega Nights: The Ballad of Ricky Bobby* were all filmed at Charlotte Motor Speedway. The track was also the first motorsports facility to host a world premiere of a major motion picture with the animated film *Cars* in 2006.

CHARLOTTE MOTOR SPEEDWAY

Concord, North Carolina

Date Opened: 1960
Capacity: 86,000

opened it in 1960. NASCAR hosts major races there twice a year, including the Coca-Cola 600, which is typically held on Memorial Day weekend.

In the spirit of making Charlotte a great place to race, a permanent lighting system was installed in 1992 to allow for night racing. The system uses mirrors to imitate daylight without glare or shadows. Charlotte became the first modern superspeedway to host night racing.

Since 1987 the track has been the site of a 70-lap all-star race featuring the previous season's winners. Originally called The Winston, it has produced numerous memorable moments.

Because of Charlotte's top-notch lighting, drivers can speed around the track even at night.

Coming into 1989's race, Darrell Waltrip was a driver who fans loved to hate. Rusty Wallace was a young driver looking to leave his mark. Waltrip led with a couple laps to go when

Wallace's car touched Waltrip's left rear, causing Waltrip's car to smoke and spin toward the infield grass. The move was known as "The Tide Slide," because the laundry detergent's logo was all over Waltrip's car as a primary sponsor.

On the final lap of the 1992 Winston, Dale Earnhardt Sr., Kyle Petty, and Davey Allison were battling for the checkered flag. Earnhardt was in the lead. As Petty tried to pass on the inside on the backstretch, his car nudged the left rear of Earnhardt's car. Petty took over the lead when Earnhardt spun sideways toward the outside wall. Allison came from third and passed Petty just before the finish line. Just as Allison won, the two cars touched and Allison hit the outside wall.

With exciting finishes, great views, and some of the best fan experiences, Charlotte earns its spot on the ultimate NASCAR road trip and a place as many fans' favorite track.

BRISTOL MOTOR SPEEDWAY

NASCAR drivers have compared driving around the 36-degree turns at Bristol Motor Speedway to driving a speedboat around a toilet bowl. As one of the smallest tracks, the high-banked oval track has steep and tight corners. Bristol is known as "the world's fastest half-mile" because cars can turn laps in a matter of 15 seconds.

The track opened in 1961. At the time it was known as Bristol International Speedway. Carl Moore, Larry Carrier, and R. G. Pope wanted to build a short track in the foothills of Tennessee. The speedway was built on a site that used to be a dairy farm. Now NASCAR holds a 500-lap race at Bristol.

One part of the Bristol track that makes it so unique and a favorite of drivers is the turns. The turns curve more steeply toward the top. Drivers can take easier turns higher up, but they

BRISTOL MOTOR SPEEDWAY

Bristol, Tennessee

Date Opened: 1961
Capacity: 146,000

 The turns at Bristol Motor Speedway make it a unique and challenging short track.

have to drive farther to do so. If a driver wants to stay low through a turn, it's much harder.

NASCAR driver Rusty Wallace won his eighth of nine Bristol victories in 2000. Wallace passed Dale Jarrett with 75 laps remaining in the Food City 500 to hold on for the win. With the result of that race, he became the tenth driver to reach at least 50 career NASCAR wins.

Legendary driver Darrell Waltrip won more races at Bristol than any other driver. Twelve of his 84 career victories came at this short track. He even won seven in a row at Bristol between 1981 and 1984.

Waltrip hit victory lane many times after starting his first race at Bristol in 1973. He also earned his next-to-last win there in 1992. He had so much success at Bristol because of the way he was able to find enough room on the track amid dozens of other cars. He tried to find space so his car wouldn't get caught in crashes. Waltrip, a 2012 NASCAR Hall of Fame inductee, finished his career at Bristol with 26 top-five finishes plus his twelve victories.

6 MARTINSVILLE SPEEDWAY

Martinsville Speedway is the shortest track on the schedule at just 0.52 miles (0.84 km). Its length offers drivers little room to pass. The track is so old that it was around before NASCAR was a sanctioned sport.

The first NASCAR race at Martinsville took place on September 25, 1949. The 200-lap race with 15 drivers didn't even have a name. Red Byron led 97 laps and won the race with his 1949 Oldsmobile. Martinsville started out as a dirt track before it was covered with asphalt in 1955. By 1976 the track's owners poured concrete corners on top of the asphalt.

Richard Petty is known as "the King" in NASCAR, and he was also the king of Martinsville. He won 15 times in 67 starts at the short track. He was so successful there that he never finished outside the top 10. Petty was also the youngest winner at Martinsville, earning his first victory there at just 22 years old.

MARTINSVILLE SPEEDWAY

Martinsville, Virginia

Date Opened: 1947
Capacity: 55,000

Petty's No. 43 car made it back to victory lane at Martinsville again in 1999, but this time with the King as a team owner instead of a racer. John Andretti was behind the wheel of the car and took the lead on the inside from Jeff Burton with four laps to go.

 Richard Petty earned his nickname, the King, racing his famous No. 43 machine at Martinsville's short track.

The win was Andretti's second NASCAR victory. He led for only four laps, the fewest by a Martinsville race winner.

Tragedy also has struck the track. In October 2004, a Hendrick Motorsports airplane headed for Martinsville crashed, killing 10 people. Jeff Gordon was driving the No. 24 car for Hendrick at Martinsville the next April. He came back from three laps down to take the lead on lap 465 and win the race. Gordon dedicated the win to team owner Rick Hendrick and those who lost their lives in the plane crash.

Martinsville also boasts Champions Overlook in the infield. It is a raised campsite for recreational vehicles (RVs). The height gives fans a great view of the track during the race. Unlike many tracks, Martinsville features a nearby forest that provides something pretty for visiting fans to look at when no one is on the track.

7 RICHMOND INTERNATIONAL RACEWAY

Richard Petty was known for his cowboy hat, his sunglasses, and his constant presence in victory lane. Following in his father Lee's footsteps, Petty had great success in Richmond during the 1960s and 1970s. When Petty started racing at Richmond International Raceway it was still a dirt track. Petty won at Richmond seven straight times starting in 1970. In all, Petty won a record 13 times at Richmond. No driver has ever come close to that mark.

Richmond International Raceway is known as America's premier short track at just 0.75 miles (1.2 km) in a D-shaped oval. It's a popular track among drivers and fans.

FUN FACT

Driver Ricky Rudd showed just how tough some race drivers can be out on the track. He was injured in a bad crash during the preliminary race for the 1984 Daytona 500. After racing the Great American Race with his injured eyes taped open, Rudd went on to win the race at Richmond the next week.

RICHMOND INTERNATIONAL RACEWAY

Richmond, Virginia

Date Opened: 1946
Capacity: 59,000

Richmond started out as a half-mile (0.8-km) dirt track and was paved in 1968. The track was then redesigned to its current length of 0.75 miles in 1988, and the race was expanded to 400 laps. In 2010 Richmond installed the largest video board in auto racing. Four massive 38-by-24-foot (11.5-by-7.3-m) video boards sit atop the 67-foot (20.4-m) digital leaderboard that keeps fans up to date. The new tower stands 153 feet (46.6 m) in all so every fan at the racetrack can see every pass attempt and every finish.

FUN FACT

Bobby Allison won his seventh race at Richmond on September 11, 1983. His seven victories there rank second all-time behind Richard Petty. Allison and Petty each started from the pole position a track-record eight times.

The Richmond Reimagined track renovation in 2018 created a more fan-friendly experience. The project included a new garage area where fans can see crews working on the cars. There are also plans for more infield suites and more hospitality areas in the infield where fans can eat, drink, and even meet drivers.

Richmond International Raceway has a long and rich history of racing. Back when Richmond was a dirt track and known as Atlantic Rural Exposition Fairgrounds, Lee Petty won the first

A huge video board is part of the Richmond Reimagined renovation, designed to bring fans closer to the action.

NASCAR Grand National Division race. Petty won with an average speed of just 45.535 miles per hour (73.281 km/h). He led the 100-mile (160.9-km) race from the drop of the green flag until the checkered flag.

8 WATKINS
GLEN
INTERNATIONAL

NASCAR doesn't have many road courses in its series. Oval courses, with their huge grandstands, are more popular. But Watkins Glen International is still one of the best tracks on the circuit. The 2.45-mile (4-km) road course is nestled in upstate New York. In 1948 a law student named Cameron Argetsinger dreamed of having European-style racing in the village of Watkins Glen. Sports cars were once raced on real roads rather than racetracks, but that practice went away after World War II. That's where Argetsinger and his appreciation for European road racing came in. He wanted to see a grand prix race

WATKINS GLEN INTERNATIONAL

Watkins Glen, New York

Date Opened: 1956
Capacity: 33,000

 Drivers at Watkins Glen zoom through the New York countryside on one of NASCAR's few road courses.

in the village with its twisting and scenic lanes and stretches. He

worked for months plotting out a 6.6-mile (10.6-km) race course

on a mostly paved route around Watkins Glen.

Argetsinger got permission from nine state agencies and even
the New York Central Railroad. The race route crossed railroad
tracks at two points, so the railroad suspended train service
on race day to make it safe for the drivers. People called that

day—October 2, 1948—"the day the trains stopped." Argetsinger finished ninth of the 23 cars.

The race moved to the permanent circuit in 1956. The next year, Buck Baker edged out Glenn "Fireball" Roberts to win the first NASCAR Grand National Stock Car event at Watkins Glen. However, in later years the track became less popular. It closed in 1981.

The track reopened in 1984, and NASCAR returned in 1986. In 1992 the track underwent a reconfiguration along the back straightaway with the addition of the Inner Loop to make the long course 3.4 miles (5.5 km) and the short course 2.45 miles (4 km). Some new turns on the track made the road course a bit more competitive and added some better viewing for race fans.

FUN FACT

In 2015 and 2017, Watkins Glen was voted as the Best NASCAR Track for the *USA Today* 10 Best Readers' Choice poll. The Glen led a list of 20 facilities across the country.

Watkins Glen may have the smallest seating of any track on the road trip, but it has hosted plenty of exciting NASCAR history. In 2012 Kyle Busch, Brad Keselowski, and Marcos Ambrose were running first, second, and third on the final lap. Busch seemed to have trouble keeping his car on the track, and he went very wide in Turn 1.

Fans get unique views of the turns at Watkins Glen.

When he came back on course, his car nudged the left front of Keselowski's No. 2 machine. The contact sent Busch into a spin on the track. Ambrose then bumped Keselowski from behind and passed him as they were door-to-door in the final turn. In a single lap, Ambrose went from third to first and took the checkered flag for the victory.

MAP

1. **Texas Motor Speedway.** Fort Worth, Texas
2. **Talladega Superspeedway.** Talladega, Alabama
3. **Daytona International Speedway.** Daytona Beach, Florida
4. **Charlotte Motor Speedway.** Concord, North Carolina

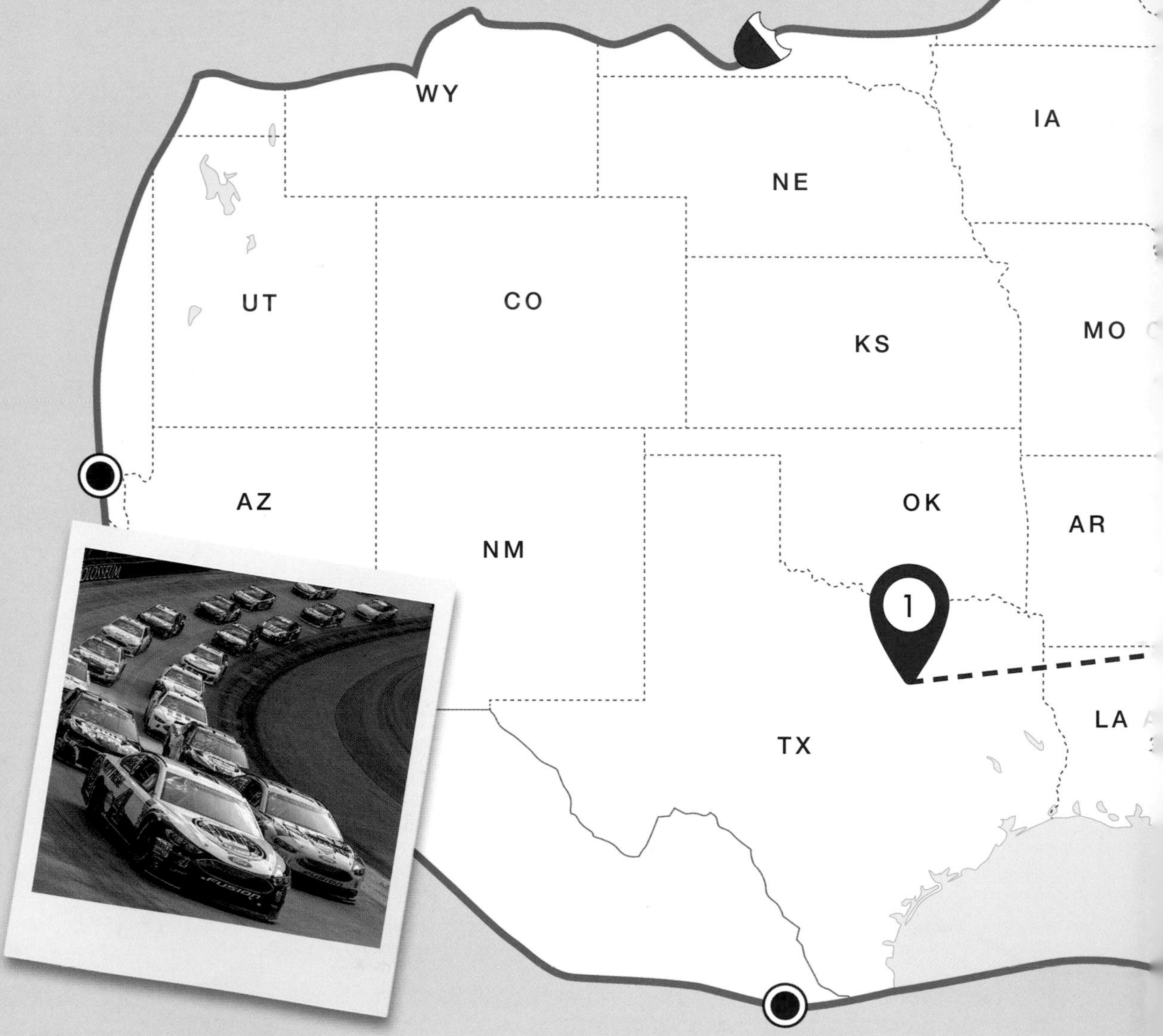

WY

IA

NE

UT

CO

KS

MO

AZ

OK

AR

NM

1

TX

LA

5. **Bristol Motor Speedway.** Bristol, Tennessee
6. **Martinsville Speedway.** Martinsville, Virginia
7. **Richmond International Raceway.** Richmond, Virginia
8. **Watkins Glen International.** Watkins Glen, New York

Glossary

banking

Where the outer edge around turns is higher to create a bend that helps cars corner.

bump draft

A special technique where a car nudges another car forward, so the second car gets pulled forward as well.

grand prix

A race that is part of a racing championship series.

NASCAR

The National Association for Stock Car Auto Racing organization that sanctions stock car racing.

oval

The circular shape of closed-circuit auto racing tracks with turns in one direction.

pole position

The most favorable position at the start of an auto race, typically in the inside of the front row.

restrictor plate

A plate that's installed on a car's engine to limit the top speeds.

road course

A closed road course designed to simulate and look like public roads.

short track

A type of racetrack that is less than 1 mile (1.6 km) in length.

straightaway

The straight part of a racetrack, usually containing the start/finish line.

superspeedway

A type of track that is at least 2 miles (3.2 km) long.

More Information

BOOKS

Long, Dustin. *NASCAR Racing*. Minneapolis, MN: Abdo Publishing, 2015.

Marquardt, Meg. *STEM in Auto Racing*. Minneapolis, MN: Abdo Publishing, 2018.

Wilner, Barry. *The Best Auto Racers of All Time*. Minneapolis, MN: Abdo Publishing, 2015.

Online Resources

Booklinks
NONFICTION NETWORK
FREE! ONLINE NONFICTION RESOURCES

To learn more about NASCAR tracks, visit **abdobooklinks.com**. These links are routinely monitored and updated to provide the most current information available.

Index

Allison, Davey, 25
Ambrose, Marcos, 42–43
Andretti, John, 32
Argetsinger, Cameron, 38–42

Baker, Buck, 42
Beauchamp, Johnny, 19
Bowyer, Clint, 14
Bristol Motor Speedway, 26–29
Burton, Jeff, 6, 32
Busch, Kyle, 42–43
Byron, Red, 30

Charlotte Motor Speedway, 22–25

Daytona 500, 4, 16, 19, 20–21, 34
Daytona International Speedway,
    16–21

Earnhardt, Dale, Jr., 13, 14, 20–21
Earnhardt, Dale, Sr., 20, 25

France, Bill, Sr., 4, 16

Gordon, Jeff, 33

Isaac, Bobby, 14

Jarrett, Dale, 28
Johnson, Jimmie, 13–14

Keselowski, Brad, 42–43

Martinsville Speedway, 20-23

Petty, Kyle, 25
Petty, Lee, 19–20, 34, 36–37
Petty, Richard, 30–31, 34, 36

Richmond International Raceway,
    34–37

Sadler, Elliott, 9
Stewart, Tony, 20–21

Talladega Superspeedway, 5, 10–15
Texas Motor Speedway, 6–9

Wallace, Mike, 13
Wallace, Rusty, 10, 12, 25, 28–29
Waltrip, Darrell, 25, 29, 33
Watkins Glen International, 5, 38–43

About the Author

Heather Rule is a writer, sports journalist, and social media coordinator. She has a bachelor's degree in journalism and mass communication from the University of St. Thomas.